Magical
Unicorns

Explore the magical world of unicorns!

Use pens, pencils, and stickers
to complete the activities on each page.

Where there is a missing sticker, you will see
an empty shape. Search your sticker pages
to find the missing sticker.

Don't forget to press out and create
a pretty puzzle and beautiful bunting
from the card pages!

make
believe
ideas

Unicorn forest

Color the enchanted forest.

Who is sleeping? Trace the check mark when you've found the bunny.

Fairy picnic

Finish the fairy picnic.

Trace the cookie.

Sticker the jar of jelly beans.

Doodle tasty toppings on the cupcakes.

Wonderful wand

Join the dots to finish the wand.
Then count to five.

Make a wish!

Mismatch

Circle the one that doesn't belong in each row.

Midnight magic

Color the magical unicorn.

How many stars can you count? Write the answer. ....

Horseshoe havoc!

Draw a line to match each unicorn to the correct colored horseshoe.

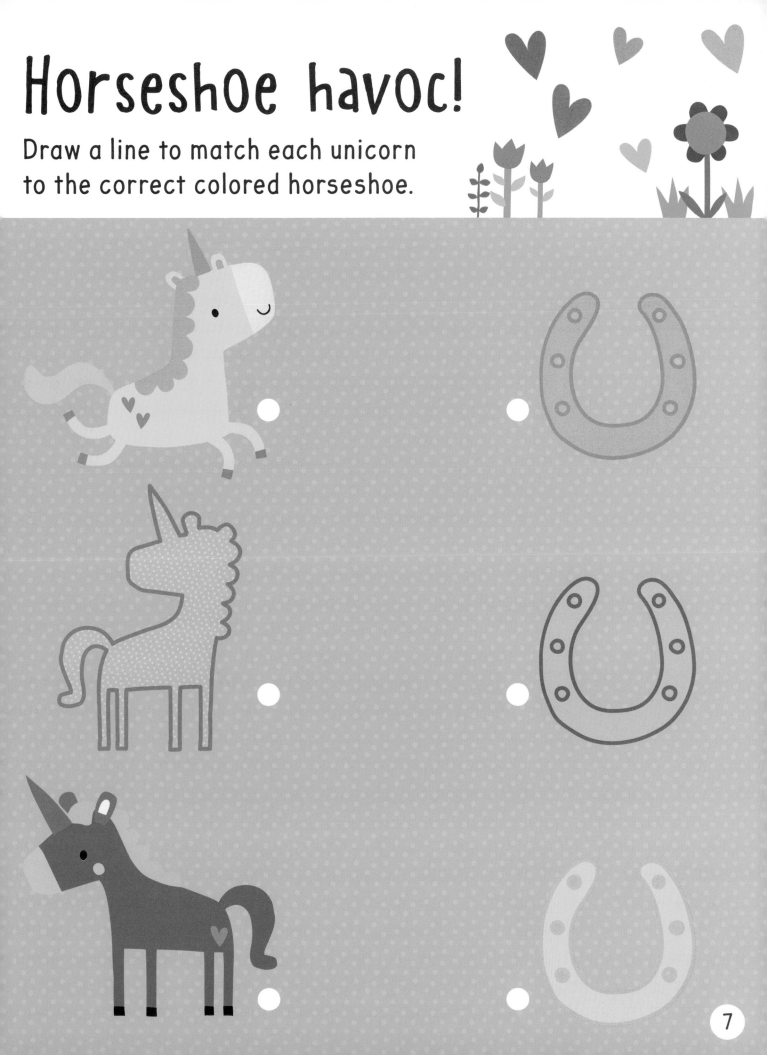

Palace paths

Use a pencil to trace the path to the unicorn palace.

Start here!

How many strawberries can you count? Write the answer. ....

Flower sums

Count the flowers to finish the sums.

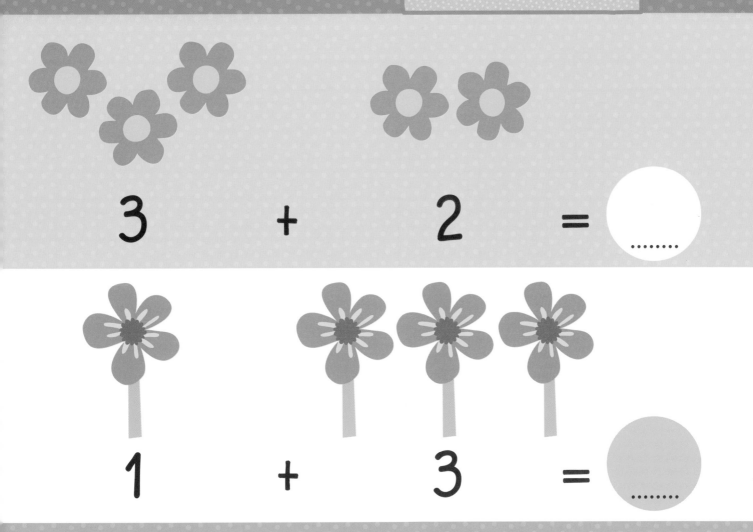

3 + 2 = ...

1 + 3 = ...

2 + 3 = ...

Fairy folk

Find three differences between the scenes.

Sticker the star when you have finished and say, "I did it!"

Tangled trails

Follow the lines to see who is going to the palace.

Unique unicorns

Use color and stickers to finish the page.
Say the colors as you go!

blue

yellow

red

green

13

Pamper day

Trace the lines to finish the horn.
Then color it in.

Sticker the nail polish to finish the pattern.

Big top!

Search the circus for the things below.

1 unicorn   2 top hats   3 balloons

Chase the rainbow

Finish the rainbow. Use the colored dots as a guide.

Picture perfect

Press out the puzzle pieces and mix them up. Then put the pieces back together to make this picture.

les.
e them
ou want!

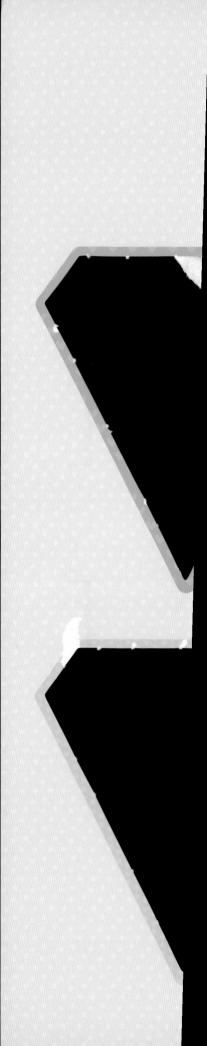

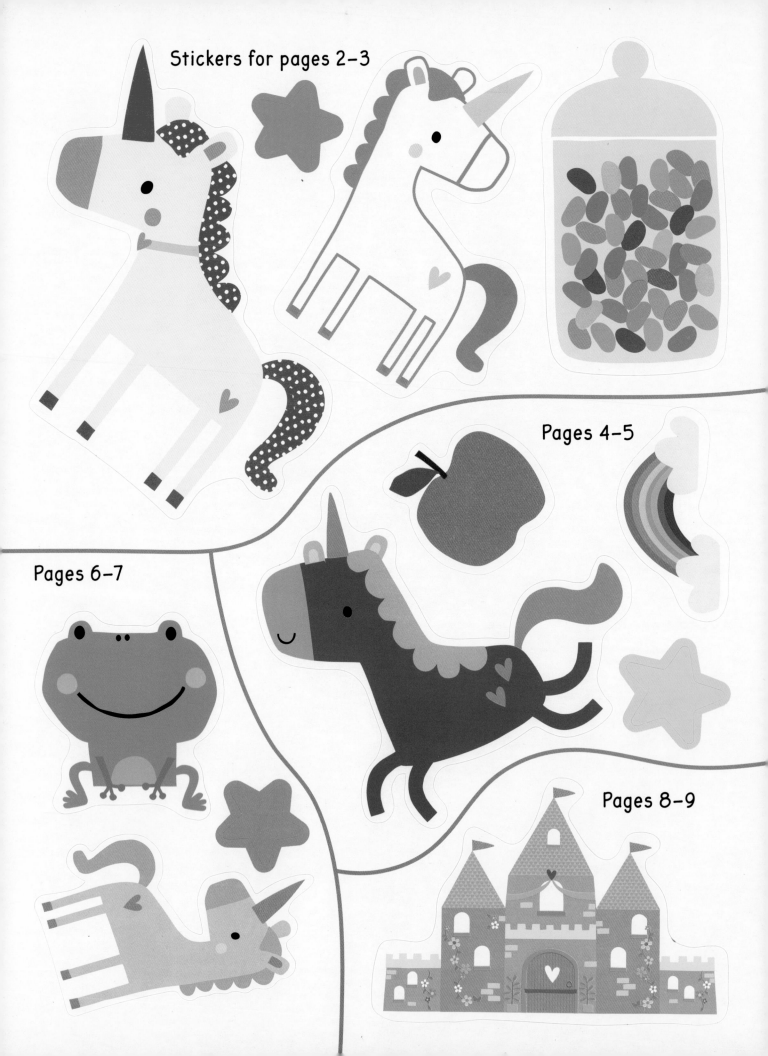

Stickers for pages 2-3

Pages 4-5

Pages 6-7

Pages 8-9

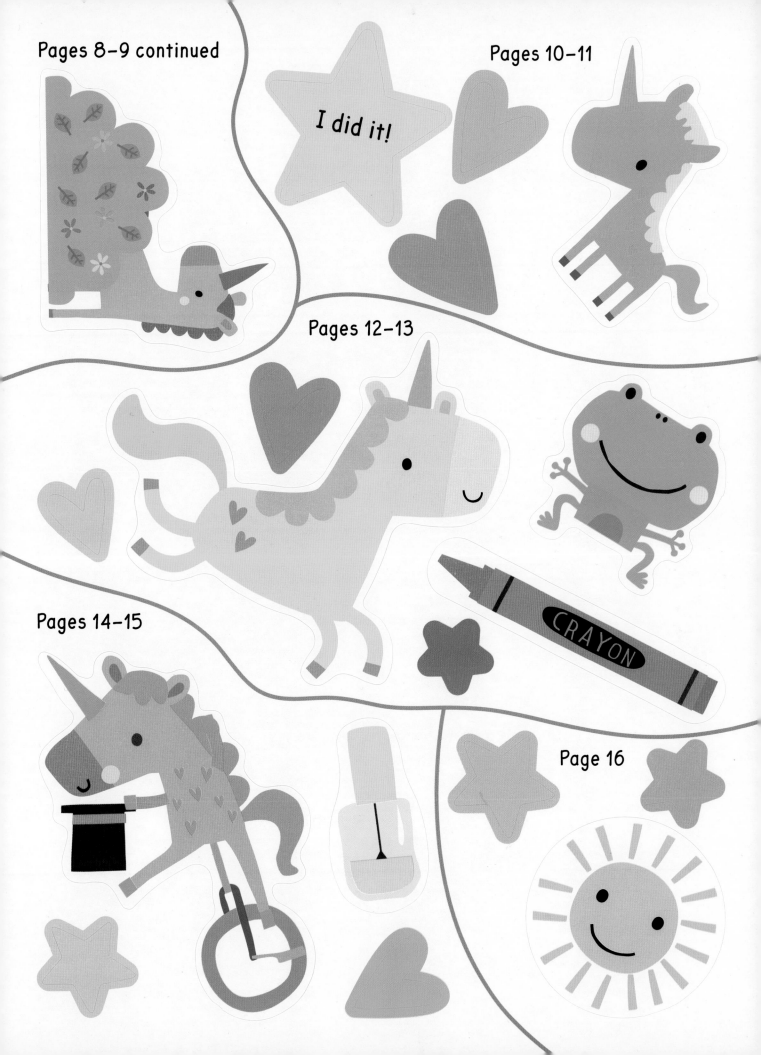

Pages 8-9 continued

Pages 10-11

I did it!

Pages 12-13

Pages 14-15

CRAYON

Page 16

Mermaid Lagoon

Dive into the world of magical mermaids!

•

Use pens, pencils, and stickers
to complete the activities on each page.

•

Where there is a missing sticker, you will see
an empty shape. Search your sticker pages
to find the missing sticker.

Don't forget to press out and create
some beautiful jewelry and cool
pencil toppers from the card pages!

Musical mermaid

Follow the lines to see
who plays the trumpet!

Shiny scales

Decorate the mermaid's tail with beautiful colors.

Pearl lagOOn

Search the underwater
scene for the things below.

1 mermaid   2 seahorses   3 sea stars

Jolly jellyfish

Trace the lines to finish the jellyfish. Then color them in.

Circle the anchor that doesn't belong.

Color me!

Color the
seahorse green.

Color the
sea star yellow.

Color the
crab red.

Sticker a white
pearl in the oyster.

Clever quiz

Circle the pictures to answer the questions.

Which mermaid has pink hair?

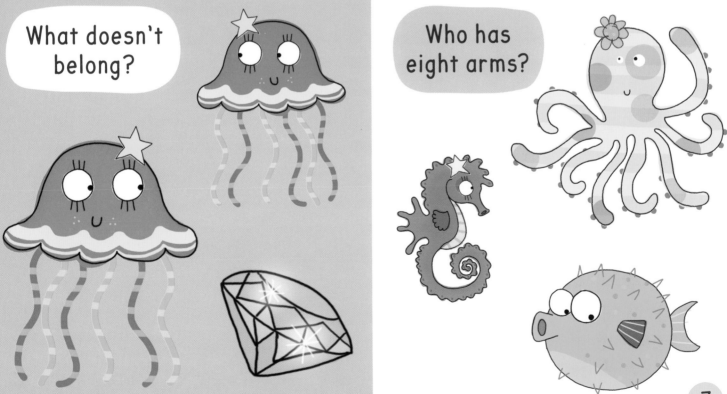

What doesn't belong?

Who has eight arms?

Find the difference

Find three differences between the scenes.

Sticker the star when you have finished and say, "I did it!"

Mermaid makeover

Finish the mermaid's makeover.

Trace the charm.

Color the perfume.

Sticker
the purse.

Cool crown

Join the dots to finish the crown.
Then count to five.

Color the fish.

1 •   3 •   5 •

2 •   4 •

Sticker a pink jewel to finish the pattern.

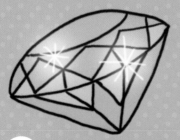  

Mer-maze

Use a pencil to trace the path to the castle.

Start here!

Friendly fish

Draw lines to match the animal friends.

Mermaid math

Count the fish to
finish the sums.

3 + 1 = ...

1 + 4 = ...

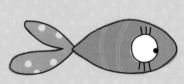 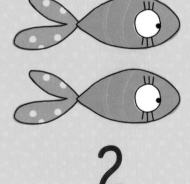

1 + 2 = ...

Underwater palace

Color the magical underwater scene.
Use the colored dots as a guide.

Can you see five fish?
Trace the check mark
when you've found them.

15

Perfect party

Trace the party decorations.
Then color them in.

Color the
ice-cream
sundae.

Hidden treasure

Press out the necklaces and bracelets.
Then ask an adult to thread some ribbon
through the holes and tie the ends together.

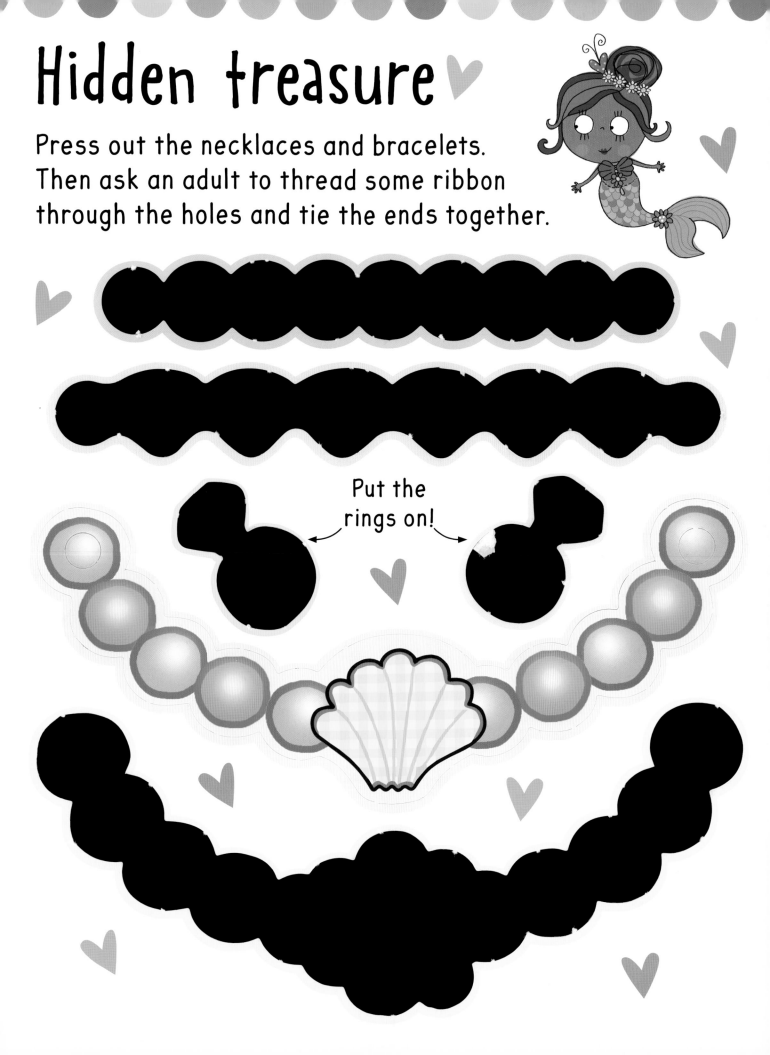

Put the
rings on!

Tail toppers

Press out and attach the card toppers to your pencils like this.

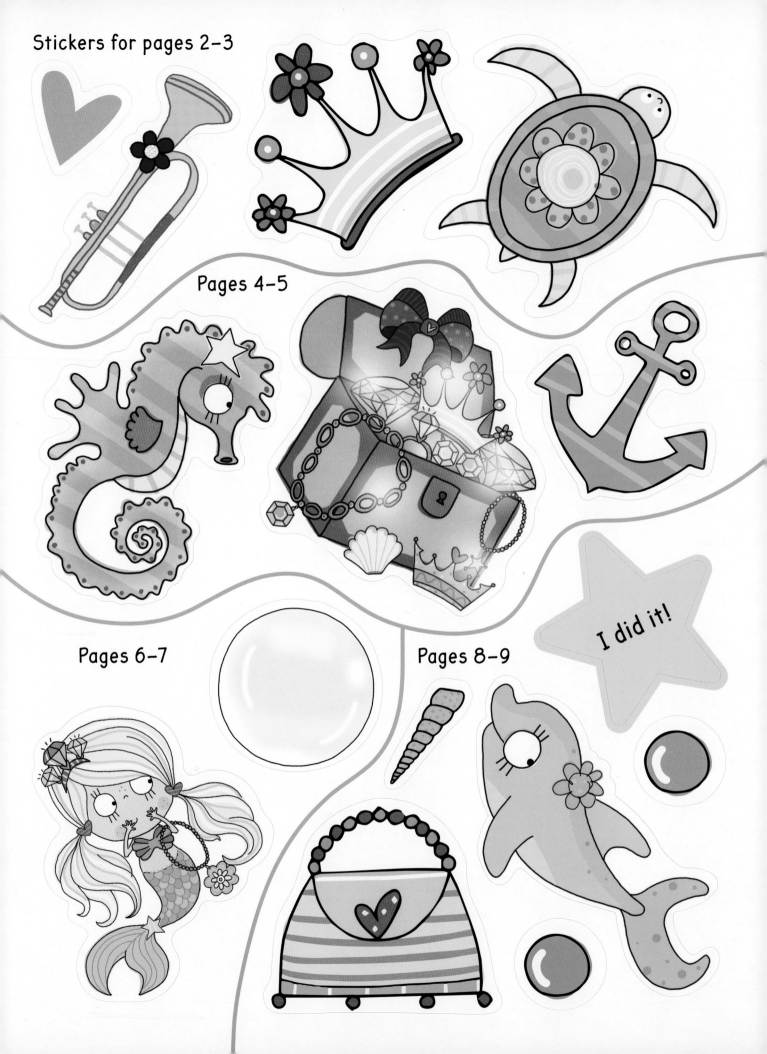

Stickers for pages 2–3

Pages 4–5

Pages 6–7

Pages 8–9

I did it!

Pages 10–11

Pages 12–13

Pages 14–15

Page 16

Princess Palace

Come and play with the princesses!

•

Use pens, pencils, and stickers
to complete the activities on each page.

•

Where there is a missing sticker, you will see
an empty shape. Search your sticker pages
to find the missing sticker.

Don't forget to press out and create
cute characters and a scene to play
with from the card pages!

Princess palace

Finish the princess palace.

How many birds can you count? Write the answer.

....

Belle of the ball

Help the princess get ready for the ball.

Trace the purse.

Color the ring.

Sticker the shoes.

3

Mismatch

Circle the one that doesn't belong in each row.

Dancing queen

Trace the dancers' trails with your finger.

Where is the poodle?
Trace the check mark when you've found her.

Masked ball

Use color and stickers
to decorate the mask.

Find the difference

Find three differences between the scenes.

Sticker the star when you have finished and say, "I did it!"

Escape the tower

Use a pencil to trace the path to the knight.

Start here!

How many dragons can you count? Write the answer. ....

Princess pets

Follow the lines to see who has a pet goldfish!

Royal garden

Count the things in the garden to finish the sums.

1 + 2 = ...

2 + 3 = ...

3 + 1 = ...

Brilliant bakes

Join the dots to finish the cake.
Then color the tasty treats.

If the shoe fits!

Draw lines to match the shoes.

Colorful toys

Color the teddy bear yellow.

Color the ball green.

Color the teacup blue.

Sticker the pink drum.

Counting fun

Use stickers and color to finish the page. Then count to five!

1 one
limo

2 two
dresses

3 three
ponies

4
four

princes

5
five

crowns

15

Happily ever after

Color the carriage. Use the colored dots as a guide.

Cute characters

Press out the characters and shade the reverse sides.
Then slot them into the stands.

stand

Perfect palace

Press out the palace. Then fold along the lines to make it stand up.

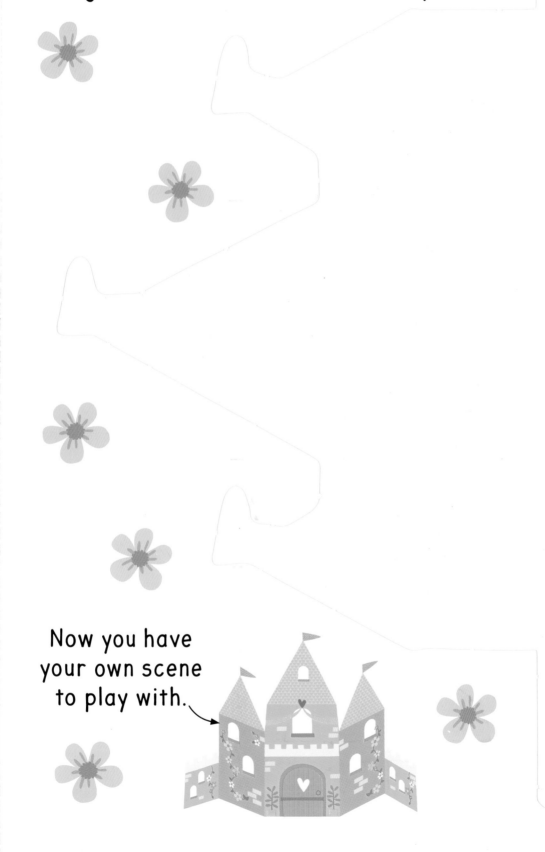

Now you have your own scene to play with.

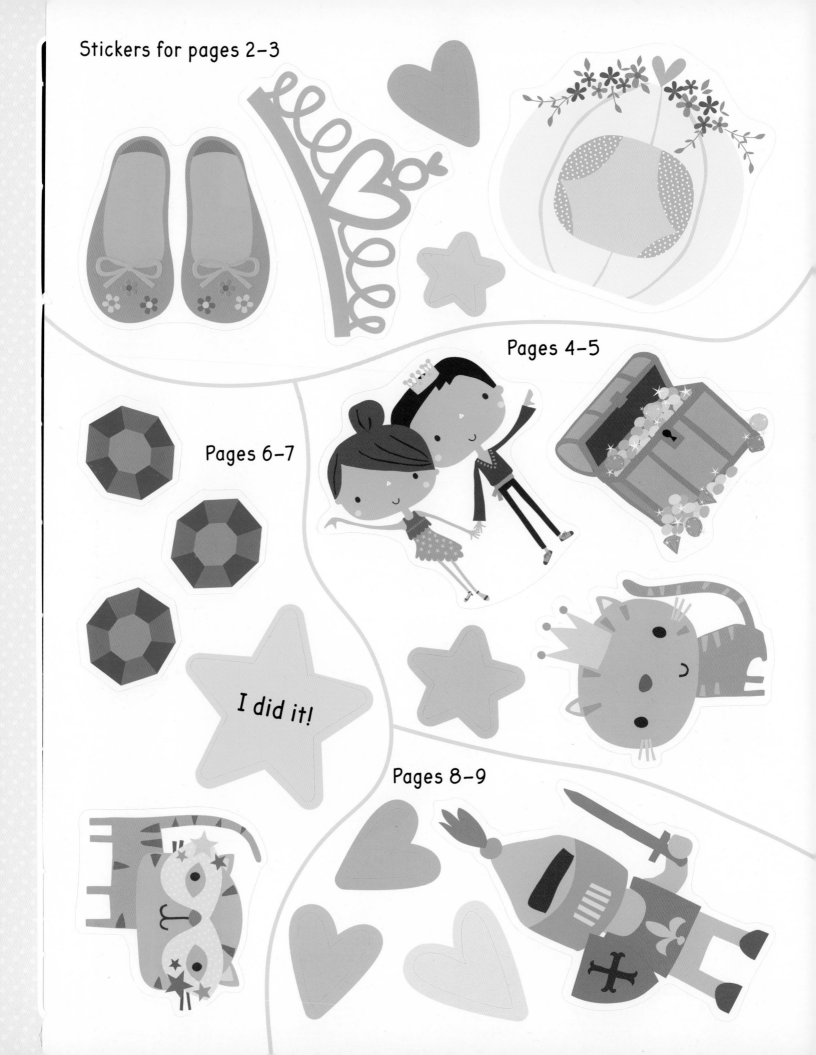

Stickers for pages 2-3

Pages 4-5

Pages 6-7

I did it!

Pages 8-9

Pages 8–9 continued

Pages 10–11

Pages 12–13

Pages 14–15

Page 16

Ballet
Show

Twist and spin with the ballerinas
as they get ready for their best show yet!

•

Use pens, pencils, and stickers
to complete the activities on each page.

•

Where there is a missing sticker, you will see
an empty shape. Search your sticker pages
to find the missing sticker.

Don't forget to press out and create
dancing ballerinas and a sweet stage
from the card page!

Dance-school dash

Use a pencil to trace the path to the dance school.

Start here!

How many flowers can you count? Write the answer. ....

Award ceremony

Finish the ballerina's outfit.

Trace the trophy.

Color the leotard.

Sticker the flowers.

Busy backstage

Search the backstage scene for the things below.

1 ballerina

2 top hats

3 stars

Draw yourself in the mirror.

Color the cat.

4

Mismatch

Circle the one that doesn't belong in each row.

Dressing room

Find three differences between the scenes.

Sticker the star when you have finished and say, "I did it!"

Colorful costumes

Color the tutu blue.

Color the shoes yellow.

Color the bow green.

Sticker the pink ballet dress.

Dance tour

Color and sticker to finish
the ballerina tour.

BALLERINAS ON TOUR

Can you find the dog?
Trace the check mark
when you've found him.

Fairy forest

Count the things in the forest to finish the sums.

2 + 3 = ...

2 + 2 = ...

2 + 1 = ...

Tricky trails

Trace the ballerina trails
with your finger.

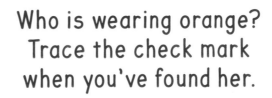 Who is wearing orange?
Trace the check mark
when you've found her.

Ballet bags

Finish the kit in the ballet bags.

WATER

Perfect pairs

Draw a line to match each dancer to their partner.

Teatime

Trace the lines to finish the dancer's cups.
Then sticker some tasty treats.

Set the scene

Use colors to finish the set for the ballerina show!

How many ballerinas can you count? Write the answer.

....

15

Take a bow!

Finish the fairy costume using color and stickers.

Can you count five roses? Trace the check mark when you've found them.

16

Beautiful ballerinas

Press out the ballerinas and shade the reverse sides.
Then put your fingers through the holes to make the
ballerinas dance!

Perfect props

Press out the scene and props. Then fold along the lines to make them stand up.

Now you have your own scene to play with.

Stickers for pages 2–3

Pages 4–5

DANCE SCHOOL

Pages 6–7

I did it!

Pages 8–9

Pages 10–11

Ballet Tonight!

Pages 12–13

Pages 14–15

Page 16